Basic Dog Train

Guide to Raising an Obedient a
Dog, Forming a Bond and Training that Dog
Through the Use of Positive Reinforcement to
Execute Every Command (With Tips & Tricks)

By Norman Thornton

Table of Contents

Thank you for purchasing this book and I hope that you will enjoy it and find it useful for training your furry friend. If you will want to share your thoughts on this book, you can do so by leaving a review on the Amazon page. It helps me out a lot.

Introduction

Isn't getting a new dog nice? Dogs are man's best friend for a reason and dogs usually become a part of a family. It is important to know to train the dog to be obedient, grounded and non-problematic in order for him to continue being a part of the family for years to come.

Do you want to know how to make a dog sit or to stop when you want him to do so? This can all be learned through dog training. It is important to start training your dog properly early on since then he will be most open to learning and more agreeable as opposed to the dogs that are older and that have traces of previous training.

The most crucial command would be for your dog to sit down and to come to you regardless of the situation whether your dog is in a competition or just being taken out for his daily walk. By training your dog properly, you can let him off the leash a little without worrying that he will embarrass you during the walk.

Teaching the dog to follow you is pretty basic, but it requires some patience to get the hang of things. You want to lure the dog to yourself while you are holding a dog treat and while you are using a gesture for calling, and when he comes to you, you want to reward him with a treat so that he learns that coming to you is a good thing and that he associates it with a gesture. Do this a couple of times a day until the dog learns that this is something he should do more often.

In order to teach the dog to sit, you should make him come to you, place your hand on his back and slightly push him down while telling him to sit. When he sits down, reward him with a treat. This is a form of positive reinforcement. If you want for the dog to sit longer, then just wait a little longer before you give him the treat which is accompanied by praise.

Dog training should be fun and you shouldn't have to spend a lot of time daily to be successful with it as long as you don't forget to reward your dog .properly, which is the most important part of the training.

This book will show you what you need to do in between bringing the dog home and him being completely trained.

Chapter 1: The Essential Commands

Everyone wants a dog which is obedient and calm. Properly trained dogs are happier and are less likely to cause trouble for owners and for the other people who happen to be at the wrong place at the wrong time. It is essential for anyone living in a more civilized community to have a dog which knows how to behave and what is appropriate. A trained dog is so much more fun to be around.

No matter how you train your dog, there are some essential commands which have to be taught. Those commands are the following:

- Heel command – A dog following this command walks along the side of the owner. This is how a dog is taught to walk when under leash. The dog should know how to walk at the side of the owner. The dog should know how to adjust his pace based on the owner' speed and the dog should be the one adjusting to the pace of the owner.

- Dogs have to know how to act when „No" is said to them – It is essential that a dog stops whatever he is doing when he hears „No." The dog should respond quickly to this and you will probably be using it a lot in the beginning stages of dog training.

- Sit command – When this command is issued, a dog sits down. It is pretty important that this vital command is mastered. You can combine this command with the heel command and you will know that you are doing well if the dog sits when walking along the owner's side. Once the dog has stopped, apply slight pressure to his back so that he would learn when it is time to sit. You can also accompany this with verbally telling the dog to sit, and after doing this a couple of times, a dog should quickly learn to stop as soon as you stop.

- Stay command – A dog following this command will remain at his position. By doing this, the dog will also stop what he is doing and come to you when he is off the leash. You should be combining this command with the sit command, and you can do so by starting to walk away when the dog is sitting, and if he starts to follow you, then stop and command him to sit again and repeat the whole process until he remains at one spot during the duration of sit command. It is necessary to be patient until the dog learns this.

- Down command – It is necessary for a dog to lie down when issued a command to lie down. This is important since this is how you take control of a bad situation and stop a dog if he is misbehaving.

- Off Command – Last, but not the least is the off command and this is how a dog is taught not to run after people or vehicles. The goal is for the dog to remain still when the owner stops and if the dog is still uneasy, then a slight tug at the leash should do the trick so that the dog learns that he shouldn't move if the owner doesn't move.

These are the commands every dog has to know and they are the essentials. Both the owner and the dog have to master these. Advanced commands shouldn't be attempted before fundamentals are nailed down.

If you want to strengthen the bond between the dog and the owner, it is necessary to do the training. Dogs are animals which have the predisposition to follow the leader of the pack, and you want for the dog to see you as a leader. Establishing yourself as a leader will prevent all sorts of issues with the dog.

If a dog is trained well, he should follow the commands without fear or confusion. A good training regimen should teach the dog what to do by using rewards and positive reinforcement psychology.

Chapter 2: How To Train a New Puppy

Isn't it fun bringing a new puppy home? A new puppy is always the center of attention. Don't forget to train that puppy since it will be much easier if you start sooner rather than later.

Training a small puppy can be easier than training a dog, since a puppy does 't have any previous training to speak of, unlike an adult dog who has things which he may need to unlearn. There are also situations in which puppy training can be harder.

What you have to know is that puppies tend to get distracted a lot more easily and that is why puppy training sessions shouldn't be too long. You want to start socializing a puppy as soon as possible. The socialization should start within the first four months because a puppy that is not properly socialized won't be able to get along all that well with other canine companions and with people. Early socialization which is done well will be tough to undo and it will go a long way.

It is necessary for a dog to be properly socialized so that the aggression would be under control and that there wouldn't be issues with other dogs. A dog that isn't properly socialized and under control is a hazard to other people and other animals. It is necessary to encourage the dog to play with other dogs so that they could learn what is appropriate and what isn't. A well-socialized puppy will know how to be around other people or animals without being fearful or aggressive.

Puppies naturally learn the proper behavior from the mother, however, a lot of puppies are separated from mothers before this can happen and that is why it is important not to neglect playtime to the puppy. The puppy needs new experiences and new places as a part of the training in order to develop.

There are pet stores which actually allow for people to bring their puppies along so that the puppies could get accustomed to new things and to actually move the socialization along. It is necessary first to assure yourself that the particular pet store actually allows for pets to be brought over so that you wouldn't be wasting time. It is necessary to allow the socialization process to go through and to reach its completion.

Something that puppies learn naturally really early on is how to bite and how not to. It is important to teach the puppy not to bite out of fear. This is learned when playing with other puppies in the presence of the mother so that the puppy wouldn't bite too hard during the playfighting with others. That is why you should allow the puppy to play with other puppies and there actually exist puppy kindergartens for that purpose. This is a really good way to handle the socialization aspect of dog training which is a really important aspect.

In order for the socialization to be successful, it is necessary to allow puppies to play without human intervention. The only time when owners should intervene is when trouble is brewing or if trouble has occurred already.

During the socialization, the hierarchy is naturally established, and it gets clear who is where in the pecking order. It is necessary to observe all this and to realize where your puppy is on the spectrum that ranges from submissiveness to dominance so that you could know how to proceed with training since the right approach will depend on a particular puppy.

Still, it is necessary to introduce puppies to humans as well as the part of the socialization. The puppy kindergartens can actually take care of this as a part of their work and they will bring puppies in contact with other people. It is ideal if the puppy comes in contact with people of all ages and gender and race.

The puppy should also be introduced to some other animals completely, which is especially important for multi-pet households. In the same way, the sooner the introduction occurs in a puppy's life, the better the results will be. It can be a good idea to first introduce the puppy to a new animal via its smell by using the bedding of that animal. The puppy will likely accept the animal after getting accustomed to the smell.

Puppy should also be taught by using positive reinforcement and rewards for good behavior so that some behaviors that are good can be learned while the others are unlearned. It is fine and cute for a little puppy to jump on other people, but not so much after he is grown. The environment of the puppy should be designed to accommodate positive reinforcement learning. A puppy which is well socialized will be able to adapt and he won't get stressed out by something out of the ordinary such as a visit to a friend's house.

As far as potty training, positive reinforcement can be used for this too so that the puppy would associate doing potty only with certain surfaces such as asphalt so that he wouldn't mess up any other surfaces like the ones inside a house.

It is necessary to be aware of timing and to only get a new puppy during the times when all members of the family can be present and when times are calm, unlike the holidays. Holidays are a pretty bad time for getting a puppy since the distractions will be all around and it will all be way too much for a puppy take in.

If your home has multiple stories, then you need to teach the puppy how to use the stairs. Puppy will likely be afraid of the stairs, and that is why it will be necessary to be patient and to start at the bottom of the stairs in order to build the confidence of a puppy.

The owner should participate in every part of teaching the dog how the stairs work by climbing up the first stair first himself. Treats and toys can be used to add some positive reinforcement. It is necessary to take this process slowly until the puppy can climb up the first stair by himself. The confidence is built here one step at a time and things shouldn't be rushed.

The puppy has to also get used to wearing a collar, and it is necessary to have patience here since this will be a new concept to puppies and they will try to get rid of it. If you want to increase the chance of puppy accepting the collar, make sure that the collar fits him well. The license and identification tag should always be a part of the collar so that puppy can be identified if he's lost and found.

Even if the collar is a good fit, the puppy will still try to get it off and it is necessary just to ignore it since acting soothing will only encourage this kind of bad behavior. It is a good idea to add in some diversions as treats or toys so that getting used to collar gets easier.

To conclude this chapter, below is a checklist of do's and don't as far as puppy socializing is concerned.

Puppy Socialization Do's and Don'ts

Puppy socialization do's:

- Do what you can to make socializing events as enjoyable as you can since it is hard to undo the effects of a bad first experience with something. Worst case scenario would be the development of a phobia that would last for a lifetime. It is a lot safer to deploy patience.

- Invite your friends over so that they could see the puppy since it will be good for the puppy if he can experience a variety of people from different backgrounds. It is a bonus if those friends can bring their own pets since it will be very helpful for the puppy to meet various animals and to learn to interact with different animals. That is how maturity is developed.

- Take the puppy to various places such as parks and pet stores instead of always sticking to the same route when it's time for walking the dog. You can also take the puppy to different places by driving a car and you should make sure that the puppy can look around through the window so that he can experience the world.

- The puppy should also have an opportunity to come in contact with a variety of items so that he could realize that there's no reason to fear common household items. Don't forget to introduce a puppy to stairs and collar.

- You also want to make sure that the puppy gets accustomed to basic sanitary procedures such as bathing, nail clipping, etc.

Puppy socialization don'ts:

- Try to avoid making a confrontation with a new animal into a surprise for a puppy since it may lead to trauma.

- Don't reinforce behaviors based on fear by soothing the puppy since that would make that same behavior stick since the puppy would get an impression that he is getting rewarded for that fear-based behavior.

- Allow for the socialization to happen naturally; don't rush it.

- Little puppies are distractable and that's why you shouldn't cram too many things in one training session since their attention span won't be able to handle it.

- Don't delay socialization since the window of opportunity for socialization consists of the first 4 months for puppies. After the windows closes, it gets so much harder.

Chapter 3: Training With Leashes and Collars

You have to choose the right style for your dog in order to get the most out of it. What dog training is ultimately about is the increase in the bond between the dog and the owner. Luckily, dogs are predisposed to look for leadership and you, as an owner, should position yourself in such a position. It is necessary to remember, when choosing the type of training, that each dog and each dog breed is unique and will, therefore, require a different approach.

The owner should also know the personality of the dog in order to be able to choose the best training style and it is recommended to work with a professional trainer to make the right choice since this choice is an important one. Leash and collar training will be the right choice for most dogs and most situations. It is also necessary to know how much force should be applied in a certain situation in order for training to deliver the results.

The dog is first taught how to perform a certain behavior or action when on a leash, and when seeing if a dog understood the behavior, the leash is used to correct the dog if he is showing that he didn't completely understand how to perform a behavior. In order for this to work, the trust between dog and the owner has to already exist to the point that the dog assumes a position issued by one of the basic commands without having to be forceful. The dog should know what to do without confusion.

The leash is used as a tool throughout this process, but the end goal is to be able to command the dog around without needing this tool at all times. What is essential is that the owner gets established as a leader so that the dog would obey without having to use a leash every time. A dog that is good should earn his freedom and flexibility.

How To Train Your Dog by Using a Leash and a Collar

The most essential tools for training the dog are the collar and the leash. The collar designed for training is the one which enables the owner to control how much pressure is put on the dog when holding a leash and adjusting it accordingly. Every dog will respond to this kind of training differently and some will be indifferent to the collar at first while others will be showing resistance. Being able to adapt no matter what happens is necessary.

The collar which is purchased has to be a quality one and made of good materials. There are many to choose from, but it is necessary to choose a collar which is properly made and sturdy. It wouldn't be very fun if the collar broke at a bad moment.

You should use the measuring tape in order to measure the circumference of the dog's neck so that you could find out the ideal length of dog's collar which should be longer than the measured circumference by 2 inches. It is also important to ensure that the chain is attached to the topside of the dog's neck since this is how the pressure can be applied optimally for more control.

Instantaneous and precise pressure control is very important. Just like the dog, the owner will also have to take time to get used to the collar. It is a good idea to ask a dog trainer for advice on choosing a collar since this choice can make or break the dog training program. When everyone is used to the collar, then it is necessary to train the dog to walk alongside the owner without lagging behind nor ahead. The dog should also be able to adjust to the speed of the walk. If a dog happens to lag ahead or behind, it is necessary to remind him to adjust to the owner by applying some slight pressure with the leash and to quickly loosen the pressure when the dog does as he should.

It is necessary to mention that more adult, larger dogs may require a bit more pressure since they still hold traces of training from before. Also, if the dog isn't responding as you would like, then the collar may be too big and needs to be changed.

How to Make a Puppy Accept a Leash and a Collar

The puppy has to be accustomed to a collar and the leash before any advanced training could be attempted. In order for a puppy to accept the collar, the size of the collar has to be good and it has to fit well. A collar which is too light tends to break, while the heavy collar may cause too much discomfort.

It is necessary to measure the puppy's neck by using the measuring tape. Most collar sizes are even, and you may need to round up a number to an even one if a measurement of the puppy's neck is an odd number such as 11. So if the measurement of the puppy's neck is 11 inches, you want to purchase a 12-inch collar.

Before a leash can be used, the puppy has to get used to the collar by wearing it pretty much the whole day for a couple of days. When it's time for the first leash, simply attach it to a collar and then let the puppy walk around the house while being careful not to get the leash stuck somewhere so that the puppy wouldn't panic and create a phobia. In the beginning, the leash should be light and it shouldn't be attached for more than a couple of minutes.

In order to have more success, the leash should be used when the dog is happy, such when it's time for a meal or for playing so that the puppy would associate the leash positively. When the puppy is reasonably used to the leash, then you can walk the dog around the house while holding the end of the leash and still letting him walk freely. Just be patient and allow the puppy to get used to the leash until you attempt to actually lead him. This training is best performed at home since the puppy feels safe there.

When the puppy becomes perfectly comfortable being on a leash at home, then he can be taken outside for short durations which can be gradually made longer.

How to Train a Dog so That He Doesn't Pull a Leash off

When a dog pulls a leash off, that is the most common form of dog misbehaving. The owner should be taking the dog out for a walk and not the other way around. It is necessary to know how to keep the dog on a leash so that he doesn't become a hazard. It is necessary to pay attention when you notice the dog pulling on the leash since that may mean a lot of things from the dog simply being excited to actually thinking that he is the one assuming the leadership role.

In the case of the dog being excited, simply stay in the spot and wait it out since the excitement will inevitably pass in a couple of minutes. The dog should continue to walk calmly just as he should after this excitement has passed.

In case of the problem with the control, it may be necessary to go back to the training since the dog currently sees himself as the leader and no further training can occur until this has been corrected. It is necessary to take a step back to the obedience training and a dog trainer can be hired to do this by working with both the dog and the owner so that the hierarchy could be established.

The dog has to accept the collar in order for calm walking sessions to be possible. The dog has to be sitting when the collar is put on and he also shouldn't be squirming or moving as the collar is being put on. Order the dog to sit back down if he gets up immediately after the collar is put on. Only after the dog is behaving as he should with a collar on, can you proceed with taking him out for a walk.

When it's time to take the dog for a walk, lead him towards the door leading outside of the house with a leash. It is necessary for a dog to be walking by your side, so make sure to tug the leash if he starts running towards a door. You only want to start walking the dog when you can both stand at the door leading outside of the house without the dog rushing out and pulling you with him.

A proper walk is the one during which the dog is focused on the owner since the owner is one who should lead. During the walks, it is necessary to stop suddenly a couple of times in order to see if the dog will stop with you. If he stops with you and sits, then that is a sign of good training. If he doesn't stop moving when he should, then ask him to sit and repeat that as many times until the dog learns.

It is helpful to give the dog a treat in order to reward good behavior such as sitting down. It is also necessary for the dog to unlearn bad behavior such as continuing to walk, which can be done by stopping and ordering the dog to sit down. The first couple of walks are really important and it is necessary to repeat certain lessons, such as teaching the dog to stop, as many times as necessary.

How to Train Your Dog When He is of The Leash

The dog owner has to make sure that all the prior training was done properly before letting the dog off the leash. The basic commands, such as sitting and walking by the side of the owner, should be second nature. In order for the dog to not be on the leash, he has to know to come to the owner when called.

The dog has to be first trained in a safe environment before his leash can be taken off in a more public setting. After the leash is removed, the owner's voice is the only tool of control. In order to really see if the dog has learned basic commands, it is necessary to introduce diversions such as other people while the dog is still on the leash. You can do so by standing in your yard with the dog on the leash, and watching if the dog is trying to go after other people that walk by. If he tries to go after other people, then correct him by tugging at the leash. This should be repeated until the dog isn't getting diverted. It is also a good idea for the diversions to be varied and in many forms such as people, other animals, cars etc.

The next step is inviting a friend over which has a dog and letting the friend's dog play with your dog. When the dogs are playing, suddenly call your dog to come to you. If he does come immediately, then make sure to reward him. After the reward, let the dog go back to playing and repeat this as many times as necessary.

Next step is to take the dog to a dog park or any similar area. This area should preferably be small and cornered off so that the dog doesn't run away. When ready, let your dog do what he wants in that area and call him back occasionally to see if he will obey. Make sure to reward the dog every time he comes back. You want your dog to learn that coming to you is a good thing.

The dog should always be under supervision when off the leash and the owner should, at all times know where the dog is no matter what he may be doing.

Chapter 4: Head Collar Training

The head collar is one of the most popular tools for training a dog. The main brands of head collars are Gentle Leader and Haiti. Gentle Leader fits better, for the most part, and it can be fastened around the neck which is good since it adds an additional layer of control. This is helpful when training is done outside and in different settings. Haiti brand can ensure more control over the dog and it is recommended to be used for the aggressive dogs.

There are a lot of good reasons to use a head collar. The training is much easier if the head collar is used from the start. It is also harder for dogs to try to pull when wearing a head collar and they will generally learn to behave quicker. Having a head collar on a dog also comes in handy in unexpected situations in which it may be difficult to control the dog, such as an area which is full of distractions.

However, a head collar should only be a tool and proper training accompanied by rewards and positive reinforcement should always take the first spot. The goal should be to get to the point where the head collar won't even have to be used.

The Cons of Using Head Collars

Nothing is without its downsides and the head collar is no exception. Some dogs may completely separate their behavior based on the collar and what is appropriate with a head collar may be different when wearing a regular training collar. Some dogs will not accept the head collar so lightly and they will try to get it off and in this case, it is just necessary to wait until the head collar is accepted. Some people might immediately think that the dog tends to bite when they see the head collar even though if that may not be the case at all.

A head collar is just a tool and it is necessary to know in which situations to use it and when it is and isn't appropriate. Holistic dog training should still take the center stage. As mentioned, the end goal is not even having to use a head collar since the dog will know how to behave properly.

Chapter 5: Do You Use Training Collar or a Choke collar?

There are many different terms which can be used to describe the training collar such as choke collar, choke chain or slip collar. No one who wants to train their dog wall can do it without these tools. It is necessary to have a knowledge of using the collar properly and that is what this chapter is all about. Necessary considerations are below:

- The collar has to fit the dog well and this what will make everything easier.

- It is necessary to understand that a training collar is a reminder for a dog instead of punishment, and this kind of mindset will decrease pressure and increase chances of success.

- It is necessary to know how to put on a collar since putting it on improperly could decrease effectiveness and safety.

- The weight and the size of the chain have to be appropriate considering the size and weight of the dog.

Why a Good Fit is Important for the Collar

It is important to make sure that the collar fits well over the dog's head in order to be sure that the selected size is a good one. The collar should fit comfortably. A too light collar is unlikely to stay where it is, while a too heavy collar can fall off. If a collar is too long, then it requires way more unnecessary precision and hassle.

How to Take a Measurement of the Dog to Pick a Training Collar

The way to measure the dog's neck is to use a measuring tape and to add 2 inches on top of the measurement shown by the tape. For example, if it was measured that the dog's neck is 14 inches, then adding 2 inches and buying 17-inch training collar is the right thing to do.

How to Make the Collar Fit Well

Make sure that the chain is always on top and above the dog's neck since no pressure will be applied as long as the leash is loose. A good training collar is the one which allows for flexibility of being able to apply and release pressure quickly.

It is important to control the pressure since the dog will show resistance if the pressure is constant. The training collar should also be made of quality materials so that it is resilient since that will guarantee safety for everyone.

Chapter 6: How to Use Rewards as a Part of the Training

Reward training is the most traditional and the most favored way of training a dog. People were using a variant of reward training as far back as when they were taming wolves.

The most up to date version of reward training has already been around for 15 years. Most dog lovers prefer reward training, although also incorporating a leash and a collar will bring forth optimal results. Each dog is different and for some, the leash and collar approach will work better while for others, reward training would be ideal. Most dogs actually fit somewhere in the middle between leash and collar training and reward training.

The most popular variant of reward training is clicker training and this can be a good solution for many dogs. Clicker training is an extension of positive reinforcement and it works by using a clicker to create a clicking sound when the dog is receiving the reward for doing something good. The goal is to be able to, eventually, only use the clicker to keep the dog under control.

Food is the most common element of reward training, and a lot of dogs can be taught by using positive reinforcement. The dogs which are used by the police and the military tend to be trained using the reward method since that way works very well to trach the essential commands.

The reward training always starts with a lure which is a trigger for the dog to do the desired action. The ideal scenario is when the dog does the desired action without the owner having to intervene. The reward is another core component of reward training and this is anything, such as a treat of a toy, that shows the dog what is the thing he should do more often.

Reward training, if done properly, can make the dog reliable. In order to achieve real reliability, the dog has to be trained in a variety of scenarios. This is important for police or military dogs who have to learn to ignore distractions. The training that is done well will ensure that the dog's attention is on the owner which is a sign that the dog recognizes his leadership.

Using Food as a Reward

Food is a great motivation for the dog and training with food as positive reinforcement is bound to be successful with animals of all sorts.

First. It is necessary to see if a particular food is a good enough motivation for the dog. During the time when the dog usually eats and when he's hungry, you can dangle a part of a particular food in front of him and observe the enthusiasm. If the enthusiasm is present, then the training can commence.

It is best to have regular meal times for the dog instead of having food available at all times since that will make the dog crave the rewards more and the chance of obesity will be reduced.

How to Command the Dog to Come to You

If the dog is interested in the food, then the training can start by you giving the dog only a tiny piece of that food. After which you will step back. Then you will hold up the food again as the signal for the dog to come. If he comes, then make sure to reward him. When the dog is following the food reliably, then you can add the sit command at the end of the current come command. This has to be mastered before moving on.

The next exercise is to walk the dog, and then to stop and ask that dog to sit down. When the dog is sitting, you should step away and tell the dog to stay while hoping that the dog continues sitting. When you want for the dog to come to your new position, simply call him and reward him if he does so. Do this whole process a couple of times.

The training sessions should be short in the beginning. As the training progresses, you won't need to keep giving the same quantity of food to the dog. It also won't be necessary to give food to dog every single time for coming over. The food can be given every fourth time, while simple praise will do in the rest of cases.

When the dog can come over reliably, then it is possible to move to more advanced exercises and games. One example would be taking the dog to the local dog park when he can freely play, but you should still make sure to call him over in order to keep the training going. Don't forget to hand out praise when it is deserved so that the dog actually wants to come when called.

Positive Reinforcement

Using positive reinforcement is fun for everyone involved. Positive reinforcement training is so effective that it can be used even with dangerous animals such as bears. A lot of dogs really like this kind of training.

Positive reinforcement teaches dogs what should be done by using rewards. Most common rewards are food, praise or scratching. Whatever the reward is, the proper behavior has to be rewarded.

Dogs, evolutionarily, always look for a leader who can guide them. That is why positive reinforcement is an important component of dog training because it has to be established who is the leader. The dog also wants assurance that the leader can protect him, instead of the leader being just someone who will hand out orders and tell what needs to be done.

Dogs want to feel like a part of the pack which has a clear leader. Naturally, some dogs will be easier than others to control and by watching puppies play freely, it can be observed how a hierarchy is formed and who is where on that hierarchy.

Obviously, it will be easier to train more submissive dogs since those dogs are more likely to take directions. However, positive reinforcement can work well even for the dogs which are more rebellious. Most dogs love rewards.

Positive reinforcement is also a good tool to train a dog who has problems with behavior because of the troubled past. A bond between the dog and the owner is created via positive reinforcement. Any dog can benefit from positive reinforcement. It is all about building respect and companionship instead of using coercion.

Chapter 7: Crate Training and House Training

It is necessary to perform house training well, in order for a dog to truly earn a spot as a member of the family. The dogs are actually quite clean animals and that is what makes house training so much easier. Dogs also develop habits around kinds of places where they do their urination or defecation, so it is necessary to associate those actions with outside places that are grassy or asphalty. You can still set up a training area within the house which would mimic some of those settings.

How to Set up a Training Area

Not a lot of room is required for a training area. It is a good idea to pick some spot in the house which is out of the way to be a training area. The more time the owner spends in the training area with the dog, the better. The owner should let the dog go about his business in the training area, such as eating and sleeping. The dog may, at first, urinate at that area, but when the dog recognizes that as a place where he sleeps, he will stop doing it.

The bed should be placed in this area and when the dog gets used to sleeping in his bed, the bed can be moved around the house for training purposes. Where the bed is, the dog will be by the default when the owner is not home

How to Set up the Toilet

The dog should have a designated toilet where he can go about his business when necessary. It is necessary for the owner to be present the first couple of times so that the dog learns about the designated toilet area and its purpose. This is easier as long as the dog sticks to his eating routine since then there will likely be a schedule of some sort for the toilet. The owner will know to lead the dog to the toilet when the time is right. This toilet area should be easily accessible since you never know how much control the dog may have.

Continuing the House Training Process

When the dog is used to using the toilet properly, then the training area can be expanded gradually, one room at a time. The dog has to learn to control his bladder and bowels before training area can be expanded to the entirety of the house. The dog should sleep and do everything that's not toilet related in the last room to which a training area was expanded until further expansion occurs.

How to Speed Things up

It is understandable if you want to find ways in which this process can go faster. It is still necessary to be patient so that the dog would be properly trained. Using rewards and praises after the dog uses the toilet as he should is a good way to speed up this whole phase of dog training. If a dog does make a mistake, which is likely, don't punish him since this will only confuse the poor thing.

What to Do During House Training With Puppies

The goal of house training is to establish good toilet habits early on in the dog's life. Puppies have to be half a year old before starting with house training since only then will they have proper control of bowels and bladder. Puppies that haven't reached six months of age yet should be confined in a room which is the least utilized room in the house and the entire room and the area around that room should be covered in newspapers in case of a mess.

When house training a puppy, you always want to make sure that he always has access to the toilet area. It may be necessary to take the puppy to the toilet area every hour. When the owner is not home, the puppy should be closed off in the room which was selected beforehand for that purpose and covered with newspaper. It is good to have something in the toilet area that will resemble an outside enviroment such as concrete or grass so that the puppy can learn appropriate toilet habits so that he wouldn't think to perform his toilet habits anywhere else in the house.

Each time a puppy does his toilet habits in an appropriate area, he should be rewarded so that positive reinforcement could go to work. Having a schedule for feeding a puppy will make it easier to keep track of puppies toilet habits and tendencies. It is necessary to be patient since house training can take months.

What to Avoid Doing During House Training With a Puppy

Don't punish the puppy if he does something wrong since this will only spread confusion. As mentioned, the feeding should occur according to the schedule and food shouldn't be readily available so that it can be easier to predict when it is time for the toilet. The puppy shouldn't be able to roam the house freely until the house training has reached a successful conclusion.

House training can be a bumpy ride, but it is necessary to keep the patience alive since a dog that is scared and forced to rush won't learn properly. House training does become easier over time if you are patient and if a puppy starts to develop a bond with you.

What You Can Expect When You House Train Your Dog

The house training is where the bond between the dog and the owner starts to be built. Good house training regimens are based around the dog's nature of not performing toilet habits where he sleeps. The house training does work well for dogs since it is built around their natural tendencies. Dogs are actually pretty clean animals. It is necessary to know how to read signals so that you could realize when toilet time is. It is also important to establish a routine around things like feeding times and to adhere to it.

It is necessary to be patient since house training won't be the same for every dog. Rushing things will only lead to accidents around the house. In this case, it is necessary to assess the situation and to take a step back.

When the dog does what he is supposed to according to schedule, he should be rewarded so that he would associate going to the toilet with good things. The area of the dog should not expand quicker than the dog's control of its bowels and bladder and it is necessary to be patient and to not rush the training process.

The house training always starts in a small area and not every dog will accept this in the same way since some dogs were captured pretty early while others had more time to experience freedom. The dog should actually see this area as a home and not as a prison.

It is necessary to provide a dog with something that would alleviate the boredom of the dog since a lot of problems in house training can be traced back to boredom. A bored dog can drink too much water and that would lead to more urination. An easy way to prevent this boredom is to make sure that there are plenty of toys for the dog. Playing will improve the dog's quality of sleep and playing will also make the dog feel safe and at home in his designated area.

Possible Issue With House Training

House training is good because it is designed around the instincts of the dog so that the chance of dog not using the toilet would be lower. Crate training is also designed around that. Crate training is confining the dog within its crate when the owner is not around. As mentioned, dogs are clean and they will do what they can to keep the crate clean. The only problems which can arise are due to the owner not recognizing that it is time for feeding or some other part of the routine.

If it happens that the dog is still nor using the toilet properly after the completion of house training, then it is possible that the owner left the dog confined to a certain area of the house for too long.

If the dog is actually urinating in the bed, that may mean that he hasn't accepted the bed completely as his own. Urinary tract infections, UTIs for short, are also a possibility and it may be another reason for dog urinating in the wrong places. It may be necessary to pay the visit to the vet if this is suspected.

Another possible issue with house training can happen because the dog didn't get the proper understanding because of which he thinks of his part of the home as another cage. The dog has to feel secure and that can be achieved by creating an area for the dog which encourages playing and toilet habits and good sleeping habits.

House training is necessary to go through in order to retrain the dog after that dog has been brought into your home, which is a completely different world than his previous dog shelter.

Crate Training

Crate training is as effective as house training gets and it is designed around dogs instincts. The idea is that the dog won't do anything to make the crate he is residing in dirty, and for that reason, he won't go through with his toilet habits there. Routine is crucial here since that will make things a lot easier. Every time a dog uses the toilet as he should, a deserved praise should be handed out.

A dog or a puppy doesn't require more than one room when the owner is not at home and this room should contain basics such as a bed, water and toys.

The idea is that the dog will stick to his crate, but when the owner does return home, then the dog should be removed from his crate and he should be lead to the toilet. If all this is done successfully, make sure to follow up with praise and rewards.

The dog shouldn't stay in the crate for too long so that he wouldn't be forced to create a mess there. A crate should, for the most part, be reserved for those periods of time when the owner is not home. When the owner is at home, it can be expected that the dog may have to relieve himself every hour or so. If the dog does everything according to the routine, then he should definitely get some praise in the form of food or a walk that lasts longer or better toys.

It is a good idea to write things down so that you could have an idea of when the dog does the most important things during the day, such as eating or going to the toilet, so that it is easier to establish some consistency and to know what to expect. When the dog understands all the rules, then he gets access to the whole house.

Possible Problems With Crate Training

Accidents happen and it wouldn't be fair to punish the dog or a puppy because of it. The best thing to do would be to simply clean it up. One possible cause of the problem is the fact that the dog has gained too much freedom too fast. The dog has to develop good enough control of the bladder and the bowels. If there are mistakes, then there was likely some misstep with crate training, so it is necessary to take a step back and realize what was overlooked during the process.

Chapter 8: Training a Dog to be Obedient

Training a dog to be obedient is crucial since those dogs are happy and they do not endanger anyone, unlike the dogs that aren't trained and which can be a hazard. The dogs are hard wired to search for a leader. What mustn't be allowed is for dogs to think that they are the leader. Obedience training is all about forming a bond between the owner and a dog. The only way to truly achieve this kind of bond is through good leadership.

Obedient dogs know what can and what can't be done. The dog should be properly trained in all the basic commands that were discussed in chapter 1 such as heeling, stopping and all the rest.

The dog should also know what is bad and what not to do, such as jumping on other people or doing damage to the things inside your house. Obedience training is making the dog aware of where he stands in the social hierarchy. The goal is for the dog to see you as a leader.

Obedience training should be fun for everyone and it shouldn't be a chore since the dog which is happy will absorb the lessons better. If a dog is trained well, then that dog can enjoy a lot more freedom than a dog that isn't trained. More freedom can mean more time off the leash during the walk.

All dogs can be trained to be obedient, no matter if they are older dogs or puppies. It is still generally accepted that young puppies are easier to train since the older dogs have leftover traces from the previous training. Puppies do have shorter attention spans and that is why training sessions with them should be shorter. Young puppies also require more play time with other dogs.

Why Rewards are Important

Rewards are crucial when a dog is trained and obedience training will yield the best results if rewards are introduced. Rewards are teaching the dogs about good behavior which should be done more often.

If possible, obedience training should be made into a game so that everyone can maintain motivation. One way to do this is to make sure that playtime is involved as a part of the playing session.

The most core dog command of obedience training is the one in which the dog walks at the side of the owner. This command is relatively simple to teach the dog. It all starts with the good collar, and if unsure about which collar is good, a dog trainer should be consulted. When walking with the dog, you always want to tug at the leash if the dog is out of allignment and this is how the dog will learn. In the beginning, it may be necessary to use a lure for the dog to follow you.

Rewards should always be used when a dog exhibits good and desireable behavior. Rewards can range from a pat on the back, to treats and toys. More rewards are needed in the earlier stages of the training.

Rewards are always better than punishment. Punishments only lead to discouragement down the line. Some form of reprimanding should only be used when absolutely necessary to show the dog what not to do and it should be kept very short. Rewards and positive reinforcement should take center stage. Just saying a sharp „No" when the dog is doing something, like climbing on your bed, can be all that it takes. When the dog gets off the bed, then you can give him a toy or a reward.

The dog should learn through positive associations since the negative ones can be very hard to turn around. It is better to do the whole obedience training right the first time so that there wouldn't be a need to go back later. Retraining a dog, when he is older, is a lot more difficult. Dog training has to teach the dog to positively associate good behavior, in order for that dog training to be a success.

Chapter 9: Possible Issues With Dog Training

The Dog is Not Coming When He is Called

A dog has to be trained to come to the owner when called, and that is especially important in the heat of the moment, such as when the collar breaks since this is a possible hazard for anyone around at the moment. The last place where a loss of control should happen is somewhere where ther is a lot of traffic.

A dog shouldn't be allowed to run around without the owner's guidance for too long since the dog which is doing so may learn that there is actually a lot of fun in running around without the owner's interference. To the dog, the owner may seem like someone who is simply spoiling the fun with his existence. The dog may learn to associate the owner and the leash negatively.

This kind of negative association may be the reason why the dog may not come immediately when called. The dog, obviously, wants to spend more time playing with the other dogs and that is why ignoring the owner makes sense. This is not a good thing.

This can all be prevented by making sure the time which you spend with the dog is fun as well so that the dog wouldn't mind coming back. It will be necessary to retrain those dogs who think that there is a sense in ignoring the owner. The dog responding to the command of coming over is a vital part of dog training.

In order to be successful with all this, don't continue with something that is unpleasant after the dog is called back from having fun. Taking the dog to the vet after dragging him from the fun is the last thing you want to do since this will teach the dog to associate the owner with the bad things. It will work a lot better if the dog is called back to do something which is fun such as eating or playing.

If the visit to the vet is imminent, then make sure that some time has passed so that the dog wouldn't make any negative associations in his mind. The dog is always learning, and that is why it is necessary to make sure that all the interactions are good ones.

The dog should be rewarded every time he performs a command successfully. A reward in form of food will probably be the best and many dogs will respond really well to this kind of reward. Any good behavior should be accompanied by a reward.

How to Train a Dog to Behave Well

Teaching the dog to behave well is good for everyone involved in the process. Dog training is what will prevent issues and make bad situations more manageable and make sure that the dog interacts with other people well.

It is important to have an understanding of how dogs interact mutually in order to train the dog properly. Long ago, humans would tame wolf pups and when wolf pups would learn to perform something which was deemed important to survival back then, rewards were handed out such as food or shelter.

Things haven't changed much and there is still a lot of things dogs can do to benefit the people today such as helping with herding or guarding the homes. Dogs are group animals and it is important for such animals to quickly realize where they stand in the hierarchy. Once the hierarchy is formed, it is unlikely to change unless something happens to the dog on top of the hierarchy who is an alpha leader.

Survival of the dogs depends on the alpha's ability to lead. The owner has to be on top and to be considered as a leader in order for a dog training regimen to be successful. The dog will only follow the commands of the owner if he sees him as the leader. It is necessary for the dog to get the respect of the leader.

It is necessary to train a dog well since the dog which is well trained is fun to be around and is fun for all the family. A lot of people are relieved when they actually see a dog which is well mannered and not dangerous such as some other dog breeds.

It is necessary to understand the motivation behind some behaviors in order for the dog to unlearn bad behavior. It is vital to pinpoint what may be the source of bad behavior so that it can be dealt with adequately.

Some bad behavior may be happening because of the stress in a dog's life. An attempts to increase the stress tolerance of the dog should be made. Although a lot of things described in this book may seem human, the reality is that human and dog motivations are different and it is important to not confuse the two. What is shared by dogs and humans is the need to create relationships and social groups. Evolutionarily, both dogs and humans relied a lot upon interacting with other members of their species in order to survive.

How to Prevent Biting

One of the first challenges of bringing a new puppy into your life is to root out some bad behavior such as biting and mouthing since those behaviors are so common among pups. Puppies bite a lot when playing with their family and this can get carried over to the owner's family as well. The puppy has to unlearn this, for obvious reasons, since humans don't have as thick skin as puppies do.

Biting is a reflex and it is necessary to root it out of a puppy at a young age. The sooner puppies learn to control themselves, the better. It falls upon people to teach new puppies, who were separated from their mothers, about how biting is inappropriate.

The way for puppies to unlearn the biting reflex is to allow the puppy to play with other dogs. Puppies bite themselves all the time and this is how puppies will naturally learn to control themselves. If a puppy steps out of line, he will get punished for his misconduct and this is how puppies learn typically. This way, puppies can also learn to work together with other dogs.

If the puppies are socialized well, then they will work better with humans too and they will be less of a hazard and will require less attention. Dogs should be socialized well so that they would know how to handle new situations and novelty. Dogs should also be socialized with other people and with children especially since dogs can actually distinguish between their owners and strangers and between adults and children.

How to Build Trust

If you want to prevent dog bites, it is necessary to cultivate trust and this is the core of good dog training. Physical punishment should never be a part of the dog training since that will ruin any chance of trust being built. Punishment won't do anything to stop biting behavior.

It is vital to prevent biting as soon as possible since this will only get worse as the time goes on if it is not addressed properly. Biting may be tolerable for a harmless puppy, but it has to be rooted out before the dog grows into an adult.

How to Get rid of Bad Habits

Bad habits are an inevitable part of dog or puppy ownership. Good communication is required so that the dog would understand what is acceptable and what isn't. It is important to realize that dogs have different personalties and that it will take some patience to teach any dog right from wrong. Below are some positive bad habits which should be corrected.

Too Much Barking or Howling

The most common issue is excessive barking. Some barking is expected, but it is necessary to keep the barking amount under control, which is especially important if a lot of other people live within the hearing range of barks from your home. It is really not necessary to receive complaints because of barking.

In order to handle excessive barking, you should teach your dog that he will inevitably have to be alone sometimes and that solitude is no reason to get stressed out. If a dog happens to be howling when he is inside a crate, then it is likely that he has to be lead to the toilet area. Dogs have needs too, such as food and water, so it may be necessary to tend to them in order to stop the barking

If the dog is howling, then you also want to check if his living conditions are as they should be and wheter a dog is showing signs of illness. Don't tend to dog every time he is howling since then you are rewarding this behavior and he will do it every time to get what he wants. Occasional reprimand could actually be appropriate during excessive howling.

A Chewing Issue

Puppies are natural chewers and this is how they get to know the world. It is necessary to teach the puppy that this is not acceptable at all times even though that's his nature. The solution can be as simple as providing a chewing toy and to provide a variety of them so that the puppy doesn't get bored. Praise should be given for chewing on these toys so that the chewing stays limited to that.

The area in the house for the puppy should be designed in a way to discourage chewing and this can be done by keeping that area free of clutter or any chewy items. If a puppy somehow does get a hold of some item he can chew on, make sure to replace that item with a toy and to provide praise and positive reinforcement to cement good chewing habit.

Possible Bad Habits During Puppy Training and Solutions for Them

Puppies are cute, but eliminating bad behavior is the price of owning a puppy. Some of the most common issues are described below:

Jumping on other people is the most common issue. Some owners may encourage it since it may seem cute, while this behavior is also rewarded by everyone who happens to be involved. That is the wrong way to do things, however, since that same behavior isn't so cute anymore when that puppy grows into an adult dog.

You never know if the dog behaving in this way could knock over someone's kid or an elderly person which could lead to all kinds of problems, maybe even legal ones. It is simplest to teach the dog about the inapropriatenesss of jumping on people when he is a little puppy since retraining is always harder.

When a puppy does jump on anyone, make sure to slowly and gently grab his front paws and to place them back down, after which you can give him a reward. It helps if all the other people that come into contact with the puppy are aware of this rule since it would ruin things if some people provided praise while others followed up with reprimanding.

Another possible bad habit could be pulling at the leash and it is necessary not to encourage this even if your intentions may be good. Giving a dog the impression that he has a choice here will lead to bad behavior.

One tool which can be helpful for training a puppy well is a body harness, and the puppy has to accept this harness just like he would do with the collar. A goal is for the dog to walk by your side and you can accomplish this by using a toy as a lure. A collar is also a good tool to use here, but the size has to be right and it should fit the puppy well.

While the dog is walking at the owner's side, it is necessary for a leash to be loose and if the puppy happens to get ahead, then changing the direction should do the trick since this will remind the puppy of the position he should be in. When corrections are necessary, it is better to apply slight pressure instead of yanking abruptly. Apply the least amount of pressure you need in order to get the job done.

The puppy should never be the one leading and it is necessary to impart this lesson while the puppy is still small before it grows to a be a 100-pound dog.

Another possible issue would be the dog escaping and moving around the neighborhood on his own. The owner should never even allow for the dog to go off like that freely since that is illegal in most places and it could lead to problems of all kinds. It can happen for the dog to escape and one thing which can put this in motion is a diversion of some kind such as vehicles or other people. The priority should always be preventing this from happening in the first place.

The dog should never even get to the point of being motivated to escape. A dog that has everything he would need, such as toys, food and water is less likely to get bored and to go searching for fun somewhere else. The dog which has everything he needs will remain home.

A dog could try to escape if he has large reserves of energy and that is why sessions for playing should be done regularly and one of them should be done right before you leave your house so that the dog wouldn't think of anything funny while you are gone.

The act of escaping should also be made as impossible as it can get by using a fence which would even extend below the ground so that the dog couldn't dig his way out. The fence should be high enough so that the dog can't jump over and if you really wan't some certainty, then just make it impossible to get out of the house while you are away.

How to Train a Dog to Behave Properly

A dog should learn to behave as early as possible. The dog has to learn which behavior is appropriate and which isn't. The lessons stick best if they are taught early. Every interaction counts and it is necessary to be certain that the dog will learn the right things.

It is necessary to know which strategies to use for training a dog since you want the dog which is loving and fun to have around instead of one which is like a ticking time bomb.

No animal in history has been domesticated longer than the dog and that is why there exists a strong bond between people and dogs, unlike any others. This bond makes training dogs that much easier.

Everyone who wants to have a dog has to understand that dogs are group animals which need hierarchy in order to function. The knowledge about this hierarchy can be put to use by establishing yourself as a leader since dogs always do look for someone to take a lead and who will provide directions and guidance. The leader provides protection in return for the cooperation of followers.

This kind of hierarchical structure is what has allowed dogs to stay around for so long. In order for the dog to follow you, you have to position yourself as a leader and that is the only way of achieving success with the dog training program.

Respect of the dog has to be earned over time and earning respect is essential in order to make some serious progress with the dog training regimen. You don't want to base the dog training on fear since that is only a short term approach and it isn't possible to last in the long run while doing so. As usual, you want to reward the dog for behavior that is good so that the same behavior would be performed again and again.

The dog should have a choice between the correct and the wrong thing to do, and he should be rewarded when he makes the right choice. One example for a dog that likes to chase after motorcycles, would be to stand near the road with the dog on the leash and ordering the dog to sit back down if he attempts to go after a motorcycle which passes by. When the dog sits down instead of trying to chase motorcycles, then make sure to follow up with praise and rewards. The dog should quickly learn right from wrong this way.

Chapter 10: Dog Training Advanced Course

An easy way to avoid any trouble is to have a dog which is trained in a way that he comes back to the owner when he is called. A dog that is well trained simply has more options and can enjoy a greater variety of locations. The dog can be trained to come to the owner by using positive reinforcement and praises and this is fairly simple to accomplish.

After the basics have become easy, it is possible to have fun with challenges and this when training can become fun. This is a good way to keep things fresh and to keep everyone continuously motivated.

The dog's motivation should be reasonably high before trying anything more advanced. This can be tested by simply dangling a piece of dog's food in front of the dog, and if the dog ends up excited, then you can move on with the training.

The games which can be played are based on treats. One example of a game would be playing hide and seek by using pieces of the food which the dog is fond of. The other possible game, which a lot of dog trainers recommend, is to have multiple people involved who will all share the lead of the dog, and the goal is for the dog to go to any person which happens to call him. This way, the dog can learn to be flexible and to recognize who is taking the lead at a particular moment.

When this game is first played, it is best to play inside a safe area, such as the owner's yard which is fenced of. The game is played in a way that everyone involved has a treat such as a piece of food, and people alternate between who will call the dog and tell him to sit down. After the dog does as he should, a treat should be given and dogs really do enjoy this. Another variant of this game would be hide and seek inside a house where participants are spread out of sight. When someone calls the dog, then the dog seeks out that person and gets the reward if he succeeds. Dogs enjoy this since this is akin to their natural behavior of hunting for resources.

How to Keep the Dog's Motivation High

Dogs are distractable and that is why you don't want for training sessions to become boring. It is essential to make training sessions fun since that is how a bond is formed and how a well-trained dog is created. If you want to ensure that the dog stays engaged, then make sure that the dog actually has something to enjoy during the day such as playtime with other dogs or walks through dog parks.

You can introduce some unpredictability by calling a dog all of sudden, and if he does come and sit down obediently, then you can take him out for a surprise walk outside or a car ride. The dog will be motivated if there are rewards since that is how he will know that he isn't doing what he is doing for nothing.

How to Make a Dog Immune to Diversions

It is important to prepared for distractions during training. During the training, the dog should ignore everything other than the training. One example of this is letting the dog play with other dogs as usual, but suddenly calling him to come back to you. When the dog comes, reward him with praise and let him go back to playing. When this is done a couple of times, the dog will learn that listening to you leads to good outcomes.

Distraction training is a pretty tough aspect of dog training and it is normal if you don't do it right immediately. This is hard because the dog is asked to act against his nature by leaving the pack. A lot of dogs won't be too happy to go along with this. You need some creativity to be successful with this and one trick you can use is to use a toy as a lure in order for the dog to come to you.

Using toys is fine in the beginning, but you want to get to the point where you can get the dog to comply by only using your voice and this is important since you may not always have a toy at hand.

Chapter 11: Possible Setbacks During the Dog and Puppy Training

How to Overcome Separation Anxiety

Separation anxiety is one of the most common issues in the dog training world. Separation anxiety can be a cause of things such as ruining property, too much barking, and other bad behavior.

The dog that is dealing with this won't handle being alone all that well but is important to not rush home to comfort the dog since this will make him seek attention only more by doing same things.

It actually matters how the owner leaves the house since long goodbyes can make things worse and the dog will feel more alone. The dogs in these situations often have a surplus of energy and they don't know what to do with it and that's why they may resort to some destructive behavior.

Still, it is possible for a dog to have a surplus of energy without experiencing separation anxiety and this situation can be easily resolved with a toy. As far as separation anxiety is concerned, it is necessary to give the dog the impression of safety and comfort while alone. This can also be solved by providing dogs with a toy. If you happen to have another pet already, then you can bring both pets together to make it easier for the new dog.

You can also alleviate separation anxiety by having times during the day when you play with the dog and give him your undivided attention. This way the dog will be happy and will be more likely to fall asleep when alone. The ideal timing for this playing sessions is right before you leave the house so that the dog isn't left with excess energy.

If you have some routine around leaving the house and returning, then the dog will be calmer since he will know that you will be coming back. It is all about sending a message to the dog with separation anxiety that you are not leaving for good and that you will come back.

How to Make the Dog Stop Urinating When It is Not Appropriate

This is a pretty frequent problem for anyone owning a dog and this is the most common reason for returning the dog where he came from. You should try to get to the root of the problem.

Dogs can urinate unexpectedly when they are excited, which can happen when the owner comes home. This is more common with younger puppies who lack control of the bladder. It usually isn't the fault of the puppy since he usually isn't even aware of it. This kind of urination should start to disappear as the puppy grows older.

It is best to prevent excitement urination and you do this by preventing the excitement. Know what excites the dog and then expose him to that thing enough times so that it isn't a big deal anymore.

One other possibility is submissive urination, which consists of the dog showing his submissiveness if he considers himself to be at the bottom of the hierarchy. That is why some dogs may urinate since they view themselves to be much lower than the owner, whom they view as a leader.

Dogs who do this tend to be insecure and/or with the previous history of abuse. All that has to be done is to make sure that the dog is taught a more appropriate way of showing submission, such as sitting.

The best method of dealing with this kind of urination is to ignore it since you don't want to approve of such behavior. It is also necessary to help the dog develop confidence and to teach him other ways to demonstrate submissiveness. As usual, desirable behavior should be rewarded.

If a urination issue does occur, then it is also recommended to check if the problem is of the medical kind such as a bladder infection. If the problem is not medical, then it is necessary to determine if the dog is urinating because of excitement or submissiveness and figure out the course of action which doesn't involve punishment since that will only cause confusion.

How to Train the Dog Which is Fearful or Shy

Every dog will be different in terms of how brave they can be. Watch your dog play to determine where he stands in the dog hierarchy. The puppies that stand on the side are usually the more fearful and non-confrontational. It is necessary to know which personality your dog has since each personality type is a different kind of a challenge to overcome when training.

Fearful dogs require confidence training since the dogs that are fearful use biting as a defense mechanism which is inappropriate and can get you and the dog in a world of trouble. A dog has to learn that it is not reasonable to fear novel situations and that everything will be alright. Dogs which are fearful also tend to be avoidant of strangers, novelty and certain things that are outside of the routine and comfort zone.

If you determine that your dog is fearful, then you need to correct this quickly since you don't want for this fear to penetrate even deeper. Proper socialization is crucial here, and dogs and puppies should be provided with opportunities for playing with other dogs of many kinds and even more various animals, such as friendly cats, can be involved. It is all about experiencing new situations when the dog is young so that the dog learns to be flexible and adaptable. The sooner this adaptability is learned, the better.

Everyone needs to learn to be adaptable to stand a chance in this world. If a shy behavior, such as fear, is performed, then it is important that such behaviors aren't reinforced since you don't want the dog to think that the owner thinks that the shy behavior is the good one which should be done more. A shy behavior has to be ignored so that the dog figures out himself that there is nothing to fear and that there is nothing to be gained from such behavior. It is crucial for a dog to realize this himself since that is how he will learn the best.

If the dog is a bit older, it is possible that he wasn't socialized well during first 4 months of his life which is the crucial window of opportunity for proper socialization. It is still possible to socialize him properly, but it will be much harder since there will be a lot of things that have to be unlearned. Another possibility is one of the dog having gone through abuse before, which will require a lot of patience on the owner's end in order to replace bad associations with something healthier.

The socialization for a dog which is older has to be allowed to proceed at his own pace, without rushing since that can only make things harder. It is also necessary to notice behaviors based on fear such as biting since that will make the dog defensive towards strangers. The dog has to learn that these fear-based actions are bad and the way to accomplish this is to reprimand the dog as he does more of these behaviors so that he would learn that he shouldn't be doing that anymore unless he wants to keep getting reprimanded.

Once again, this whole process has to be allowed to progress at the dog's pace and it shouldn't be rushed. Only present the dog with a certain situation once you are certain that he has built enough confidence to handle it in a confident manner.

How to Get Rid of the Fear of Loud Noises

It is normal for dogs to get unsettled by loud noises, but for some dogs, it is worse than it is for others. You should only worry if a dog has an unhealthy amount of fear due to loud noises which are preventing him from going along with his day as he should. Dogs can react in many ways, such as urinating on a carpet or chewing the furniture.

It may seem reasonable to try to calm the dog down, but when doing so, the dog is getting a reward for being scared. If the reward is really good, then the dog will think that being scared is the right thing to do and he will, naturally, do more of that. What you should do during these loud noise situations, such as fireworks, is to ignore the dog if he is visibly scared and let him handle the fear response on his own. Just make sure that there aren't any opportunities for dog hurting himself or getting stuck. You may just confine the dog to a separate room which dog happens to like if you think that will be necessary. If the dog is dealing with his fears in a room where he feels safe, then the whole process will be much smoother. This room shouldn't have any furniture which dog can get stuck under.

How to Use Diversions

A good way to distract dogs from their fears is to use diversions. If your dog is afraid of fireworks, then make sure to gather up all his toys during the fireworks. There is no guarantee that the dog will play, which is especially true for the ones which tend to be more fearful, but it is worth giving it a shot. You can also intervene and play with the dog yourself. This is how good memories form, and future fireworks may not be so scary for the dog anymore. It will take time since fear of loud noises is a pretty old instinct. Most things are born with the fear of loud noises.

How to Make the Dog Less Fearful

If there is a fear which is negatively impacting a dog's life, then it is necessary to increase the exposure to that fear so that the dog would be less sensitive to that fear. This works by introducing the dog very gradually to the pieces of things which scare him. If the dog is afraid of firecrackers, then you can start by playing the audio recording of a firecracker going off to the dog. If the dog does get scared, don't try to calm him down since that would only act as a reward for fear based behavior. If he doesn't get scared, make sure to reward him.

Fears of loud noises are still ingrained deeply in dogs and it will take patience to desensitize the dog to this old instinctual response.

How to Gain the Respect of the Dog

Nothing can be achieved before the confidence and respect of the dog is developed. This applies to many animals, but especially to dogs because of how they function. Dogs are group animals and they need a leader, and that is how an owner has to establish himself in order for the dog training program to be a successs and in order for that dog to do as he is told.

Everything is in vain until the respect of the dog has been earned. Respect and trust can only be built through patience and repetition and through good interaction between the dog and the owner. The progress of the training will skyrocket after the time has been invested in cultivating healthy respect. Do a bit more work upfront so that you would have to wrok less later.

A lot of new dog owners mistakenly think that love and caring are all that is necessary for successful dog training. Those do matter, but actually gaining confidence and respect is of the utmost importance. The dog shouldn't be given free roam to do whatever it pleases since that is how the dog can gain the advantage, which is not how respect is built. Clear boundaries are necessary so that good behavior could be clearly distinguished from the bad. This is how the order is maintained.

Dogs actually want these boundaries since that is something that the leader would do. Boundaries make it clear where every member stands and what is expected of him. Having a hierarchy is what allows the group to function in the first place. The dog will be confused and lost if he doesn't get this kind of leadership from anyone.

For training sessions to be effective, it is best to start them off with a bit of play in order to get things going. The beginning and the ending of the training sessions are what is really important since that is what tends to be remembered the most. The training will produce a lot more favorable results if the dog has positive associations which will also do good things for the health and happiness of that dog. Such a dog is much easier to work with and to train.

The training session is doomed if the dog becomes bored, and for that reason, it is necessary to prevent this by not just sticking to the most basic obedience training stuff such as walking along side the owner, sitting etc. These skills are crucial and it is not possible to advance to more advanced stages before mastering those, but it is necessary to add some variety since variety is the spice of life and the sessions will be more enjoyable for everyone.

Conclusion

Dogs which have a history of abuse and fear based conditioning don't understand their actions all that well in the first place, and that is how behavioral issues actually take form. Those behavioral issues can turn a troubled dog into a hazard for anyone close enough. However, if patience and care are applied, then a lot of this can be turned around and a bond between the owner and the dog can start to form so that everyone can benefit from this new relationship.

If you have read this book up to this point, then there is no doubt that your dog will be performing some pretty impressive tricks in only a couple of weeks. You probably weren't even aware of all the things that have to be taken into consideration when getting a dog and training him properly. Luckily, that is why books such as these exist, so that you could learn from the experience and mistakes of others. Reading books such as these is a good form of shortcut since you are cutting your learning curve short and saving a lot of time and energy by knowing what to do beforehand. Just remember to deploy patience and to use positive reinforcement in order to make good habits and behaviors stick.

I hope that you have enjoyed this book and that you will apply some of this knowledge to create a well mannered four-legged beast. If you want to share your thoughts on this book, you can do so by leaving a review on the Amazon page. It helps me out a lot. Have a great rest of the day!